T5-DHH-332

OK, Light the Candles!

THE **ULTIMATE** BIRTHDAY BOOK

Detroit ● New York

OK, Light the Candles!

All rights reserved.
Avanti Press, Inc.
Box 2656
Detroit, Michigan 48231

www.avantipress.com

06 07 08 APO 10 9 8 7 6 5 4 3 2 1

ISBN: 193395761-1

Avanti Press, Inc. (API) thanks the many talented
contributors who have created the images featured in
this book. Image Copyrights (©) are owned either by
API or by the photographer(s).

Cover: API, John Giustina/GettyImages, Richard Hutchins/
Corbis. **Inside flap:** Neo Vision/GettyImages. **To/from:** API, Renee
Lynn/Corbis. **Title page:** API, Ted Chin, Lenette Newell/Workbook
Co-Op Stock. **Light your candles:** API, Dennis Mosner. **Wisdom:** API,
Chris Trayer. **Gracefully:** Ron Kimball. **Funny:** API, Ted Chin, Lenette
Newell/Workbook Co-Op Stock. **Annoy:** Patrick Dean/Index Stock.
Glasses: Neo Vision/GettyImages. **Big:** G.K. & Vikki Hart/GettyImages.
Really big: API, Thom Lang, Harv Gariety/Rick Yearick. **Like selective
memory:** Diane Bladecki. **The truth is out there:** API, Joe McBride/
GettyImages. **Forget:** API, Dennis Mosner. **Remember:** Photo ©
Wolverine World Wide. **Forget:** API, Dennis Mosner. **Remember:** API, Brian
Velenchenko. **Forget:** API, Scott Dingman. **Gracefully:** API, Scott Dingman,
Dirk Anschutz/GettyImages. **Value:** David Langley. **Inside and out:** API, Chris Amaral.
Strong: API, Chris Collins/Corbis, Laurence Dutton/GettyImages. **Rise:** API, Dennis
Mosner. **You:** API, Renee Lynn/Corbis. **Special wish:** API, Ted Chin, Stuart Westmorland/
GettyImages. **Happy birthday:** API, John Giustina/GettyImages, Richard Hutchins/
Corbis. **Back cover:** API, Ted Chin, Lenette Newell/Workbook Co-Op Stock.

Printed in China

Getting older is not for sissies! If it's not
the sagging, creaking, or squinting … it's
what's happening to your hair!

Fortunately, your sense of humor gets better
every year. And when it comes to birthdays,
laughter truly is the best medicine.

So take a deep breath and remember
how wonderful you are. Enjoy your
'just desserts'… this is your day to have
your cake and eat it too.

Okay, go ahead,

Light Your Candles!

Our blue-ribbon panel

shares its wisdom...

...on the art of aging

gracefully!

Because getting older
        isn't always fun, but it sure is

funny!

For instance, little things
no longer **annoy** us...

Without our glasses, we can't even see the little things!

Clearly, it's time to focus

on the **big** things

and the really

big things.

Like selective memory...

You remember "the truth

is out there,"

but **forget**

where you put the car keys!

You remember

every golf score,

but forget

your cholesterol count!

You remember your *first kiss*...

but forget
what you had for lunch!

Aging *gracefully*

can be a tricky business…

but it *teaches us*
to value who we are

...inside and out.

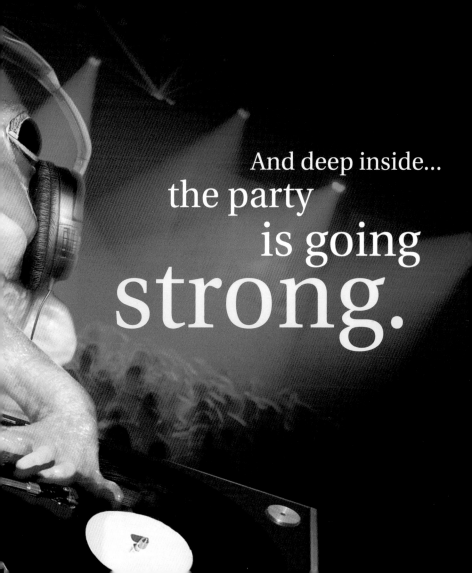

And deep inside...
the party
is going
strong.

So go ahead

and rise to the occasion...

Because it's time

to celebrate...

YOU!

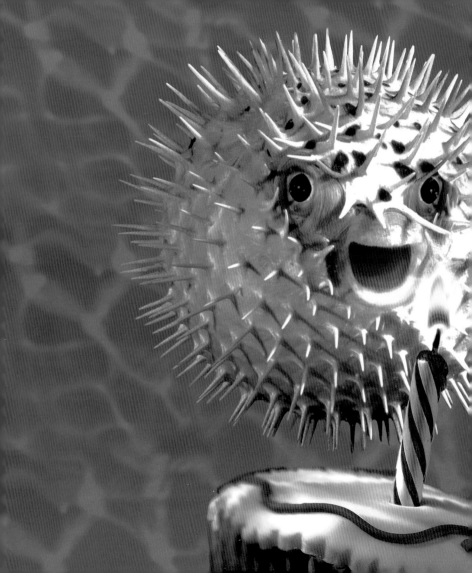

make a
special wish...